THE LORD IS OUR REFUGE

52 Weekly Devotions for Trusting God

JACK FLACCO

For the elect.

CONTENTS

PREFACE

We live in a changed world. No longer can we freely walk into a restaurant, movie theater or shopping mall without taking precautions. Although schools are open, masks are now the new normal. Churches currently have guidelines in place for limited-capacity seating, addressing regional health regulation concerns. What we once took for granted, our freedom to assemble, has all but disappeared during the pandemic.

We are not strangers to suffering. The Apostle Peter once wrote we should rejoice and be glad when a fiery trial comes upon us, for by us sharing in Christ's sufferings, God reveals His glory. If ever there were a time when we would be sharing in Christ's sufferings, it would be now. God heals all those who believe Jesus is the Savior. Whether that healing is in this lifetime or the next, He has yet to break one of His promises.

Yet, in all this, one thing is certain: God will never abandon us nor forsake us. He knows what we, His church, are undergoing; and He will never allow us to suffer more than we can bear. Whatever the trial, whatever the tribulation, His Word will always stand firm and His plan will never fail. Through His Son, Jesus, we have salvation. Under no other name other than Jesus do we have freedom from the penalty of sin.

Wonderful is God's purpose for us that He should consider us His children and heirs to His kingdom. If heirs, how much more will He do for us to make certain our inheritance. For one day, all this will be gone, and we shall dwell with the Lord forever.

May this book encourage your spirit and uplift your heart. May it provide comfort in uncertain times and draw you closer to God. May it guide you to His Word and show you how perfect His plan for us truly is. The Lord is our refuge.

Jack Flacco
October 2020

PART 1

God's Love Lasts Forever

"We rejoice in our sufferings, knowing that suffering produces endurance, and endurance produces character, and character produces hope, and hope does not put us to shame, because God's love has been poured into our hearts through the Holy Spirit who has been given to us."

—Romans 5:3-5

WEEK 1

God Keeps His Promises

God promised He would forgive us our sins. When he gave His son Jesus as a sacrifice to redeem us to Him, we would forever have a mediator, who would intervene on our behalf. No longer would sin bind us to death, but God would free us from its penalty.

> "I will establish my covenant with you, and you shall know that I am the LORD, that you may remember and be confounded, and never open your mouth again because of your shame, when I atone for you for all that you have done, declares the Lord GOD." (Ezekiel 16:62-63)

We were once slaves to iniquity, imprisoned by the flesh. We knew nothing of the Spirit; for by the Spirit, if we had knowledge of His power, we would have been free, instead of being captives to our inward lusts. Christ our Savior has freed us.

God's forgiveness is beyond measure. His grace is beyond our understanding. We may feel our sins are unpardonable, but God's patience is long and enduring. He will keep forgiving us as many times as we bow our knee to Him and repent with our whole heart.

Therefore, it is with great joy that we have God as our king. He will pardon us from the penalty of our sins, bless us with the knowledge of His coming kingdom and prosper us with the gift of the Holy Spirit because God keeps His promises.

WEEK 2

His Love for Us Will Never Fail

For us who have accepted Christ as our Savior, we have Jesus living inside us. Knowing this, we have cause for great celebration with the Lord, for His spirit is powerful, just and righteous. No evil is too great that it can overtake us. No power is too strong that it can overwhelm us. And no spirit is higher than that of God's spirit, comforting us in our time of need.

> The steadfast love of the Lord never ceases;
> his mercies never come to an end;
> they are new every morning;
> great is your faithfulness.
> "The Lord is my portion," says my soul,
> "therefore I will hope in him."

(Lamentations 3:22-24)

As many times as we cry out to God, He is always there. He listens to our pleas, he answers us in the stillness of the night, and when we are most vulnerable, He sends someone to comfort us. The fiery trial remains, but through our prayers we feel Him listening to us; we feel Him reassuring us. His word renders our troubles as a fleeting wind. He provides the perseverance we need to move forward. He supplies the strength we need to overcome adversity.

Nothing is so great that God cannot intervene on our behalf. His power is beyond measure, and through it, He sustains all things. Therefore, how hard would it be for God to rescue us in our time of need? For we can say, nothing in this lifetime is greater than the crown set aside for us in the coming age. The treasures of this world will rust and wither, but our treasures in heaven will be without end.

All glory belongs to the Highest, King of Heaven and Earth. Let all the angels praise His name, for He is good. There is no one greater than God. He reigns supreme above all things. Nothing exists He has not made, for He made all things. He is the beginning and the end, the creator of all, and we are in His image, wonderfully made, perfectly crafted.

Give thanks to God, worship Him with arms outstretched; praise Him in the fields, praise Him in the woods, praise Him in the quiet places. Give glory to the Father of all, for His gift to us is eternal life through Christ Jesus His son.

May God pour love into your heart so that you may become a perfect witness for others to follow. May your light shine in the darkness so that you may become a bulwark for those who are seeking the truth. Glorify God always, giving Him honor in everything. Never allow Satan to take away what rightfully belongs to you. Trust God, for His love for us will never fail.

WEEK 3

God Is Forgiving

God is forgiving in all things, who would not want anyone to perish. His mercies are from sunset to sunset; there is no end. He is patient, kind and loving. No matter what we have done, He is ready to forgive. God's love for us will never fail.

"I will put my law within them, and I will write it on their hearts. And I will be their God, and they shall be my people. And no longer shall each one teach his neighbor and each his brother, saying, 'Know the LORD,' for they shall all know me, from the least of them to the greatest, declares the LORD. For I will forgive their iniquity, and I will remember their sin no more." (Jeremiah 31:33-34)

If we repent and give our heart to the Lord, His spirit will live in us, and we will live in Him. We will want to forgive others as He has forgiven us. His grace will be upon us, and we will fellowship with Him in the fullness of joy.

Great is our God for having given His Son Jesus so that we would have salvation, for through Christ's sacrifice we have everlasting life.

When we believe in Jesus, we believe God will forgive us. We no longer have sin as our master, but we have true freedom, where we are no longer bond slaves to iniquity. Our liberty is in God the Father, the one and only true God, who loves us without restraint.

We have freedom to love, to be at peace, to have patience with one another, to be kind and good, to have faith, and to show gentleness and self-control. Our greatest joy comes from knowing God has redeemed us with Christ's sacrifice.

Let us go, therefore, to all the world and proclaim the gospel to all nations, for God's grace and mercy shall abound forever. In all things, God is forgiving.

WEEK 4

Preach the Gospel to All

If someone asks of the hope that lies within you, tell them about Jesus, how He saved you from the penalty of your sins. Preach Christ to all, so that you may attain your full reward, which is in heaven.

> "Go therefore and make disciples of all nations, baptizing them in the name of the Father and of the Son and of the Holy Spirit, teaching them to observe all that I have commanded you. And behold, I am with you always, to the end of the age." (Matthew 28:19-20)

The good news of the gospel is that Jesus died so that we might live. No other event in history is as important as Christ giving up His life in order that God might save us. No longer do we have a penalty hanging over our heads for the wrongs we have committed.

O how great is our God to have given His Son as a sacrifice in our stead! Freedom is ours to live joyful and meaningful lives filled with hope. By God's grace we are His elect, saved to make disciples of all nations, leading them to observe all that Christ taught.

As the Holy Spirit lives in us, God's purpose lives in us and becomes our purpose. We will want to draw others to Jesus, so that they might experience the same joy we experience when we fellowship with God. There is no substitute for His love.

Whatever rejection we may feel from those who do not want to follow Christ, is a rejection of God Himself. We have done what Jesus had commanded, to act as God's instrument in His hands. If others reject us, then they are rejecting God.

Bless everyone with the good news of God's salvation, Jesus Christ. Give them peace by giving them hope. Show them what Christ living in us could do for them. Preach the gospel to all.

Love One Another

No love is greater than giving one's life for a friend. Jesus said this and by His giving of Himself on the cross, lived this. We also ought to love one another as much as we love ourselves.

> "Beloved, if God so loved us, we also ought to love one another. No one has ever seen God; if we love one another, God abides in us and his love is perfected in us. By this we know that we abide in him and he in us, because he has given us of his Spirit." (1 John 4:11-13)

To love one another, we ought to forgive one another. True love is forgiving. When others wrong us, the spirit within us, God's spirit, leads us to show mercy on others, not because they deserve it, but because it is within us not to hold them guilty for their sins.

God has forgiven us of all our sins. If we repented and gave our hearts to Him, He no longer holds anything against us. He did this because He loves us and does not want anyone to perish. In so doing, He shares His joy with us through the Holy Spirit, who comforts us.

Be joyful, for as God has forgiven us, we ought to forgive others. By this, others will know God is living in us and us in Him; and we have hope. That hope will never fade, for God's love never fades.

Beloved, love one another.

WEEK 6

Sing Praise to the Lord

I will sing praise to the Lord my God. He knew me in my mother's womb, nurtured me, taught me His ways and raised me to speak His heart. I will take refuge in Him, for I know He will deliver me from all my trials.

> "I will give to the LORD the thanks due to his righteousness, and I will sing praise to the name of the LORD, the Most High." (Psalms 7:17)

Though the earth closes its clefts around me; though the water seeps above my chin; though the light of day diminishes into night, my God will never forsake me. He will restore my soul and save me from the hands of the grave.

God knows when I am hungry and will feed me. He knows when I am thirsty and will give me drink. He knows when I fall asleep and when I awaken from my slumber. He knows all things and will not leave me to the lions, but will chastise the wild beasts, for I am His son.

I will sing praise to the Lord my God, for He is good. I will give thanks for all His gracious deeds. His loving kindness is beyond measure. His power sustains all things. Sing praise to the Lord our God.

Great Is the Lord

Great is the Lord in all His majesty; His works fill the earth and there is no end to his glory. How great is our God that He should consider us heirs to all He has?

> I will extol you, my God and King,
> and bless your name forever and ever.
> Every day I will bless you
> and praise your name forever and ever.
> Great is the LORD, and greatly to be praised,
> and his greatness is unsearchable.

(Psalms 145:1-3)

Great is the Lord, for He forgives us of all our sins. He sacrificed His son Jesus so that we would have salvation; because of His forgiveness, we are at one with Him. No longer does sin bind us, but we are free.

Great is the Lord, for His mercy never fails. As many times as we fall, He is there to raise us to our feet. His patience for us endures forever and His grace upon our lives is from everlasting to everlasting.

Great is the Lord, for His love is as the stars; for as deep is the ocean and as high is the sky, His love for us will never depart. He will fill our heart with His spirit so that we will want to love Him as much as He loves us.

O how great is the Lord, for He is good.

Bless the Lord, O My Soul

Bless the Lord always, give him honor and glory in all of creation. He defends the weak, provides to those who do not have and strengthens the righteous. There is no one like our God, for He is merciful and will heal us of our infirmities.

> Bless the LORD, O my soul,
> and all that is within me,
> bless his holy name!
> Bless the LORD, O my soul,
> and forget not all his benefits,
> who forgives all your iniquity,
> who heals all your diseases.

Psalms (103:1-3)

We have absolute joy serving the Lord of Hosts. He has given us hope for a future with no suffering. He has given us His Son to pay for our sins, to suffer on the cross meant for us. Bless the Lord, for He is good. His grace abounds forever.

O how great is our God. We shall not feel defeat with the Lord as our bulwark. He hastens the demise of our enemies, raises the faint of heart to be shepherds and blows the trumpet to foil the evil one. Great is our God, perfect and just in all His judgments, and righteous in all His ways.

Bless the Lord, O my soul, for He is good.

WEEK 9

God Restores Our Soul

God's pleasure is caring for His sheep. He does this by the Holy Spirit, which He has given to all His children in order that we may live. Through His nurturing spirit, He restores our soul.

> He restores my soul.
> He leads me in paths of righteousness
> for his name's sake.
> Even though I walk through the valley of the
> shadow of death,
> I will fear no evil,
> for you are with me;
> your rod and your staff,
> they comfort me.

(Psalms 23:3-4)

No trial is too great and no tribulation is too strong that it would hold back God's hand from our lives. His love for us is greater. Things can change in a moment; therefore, brothers and sisters, let God's love flow through us as a testimony to those who are lost.

God will never abandon us. He will never forsake us. Our joy comes from knowing we have His love to comfort us. He will replenish the light in our eyes and apportion strength to our bones so that we can overcome daily the ruthless attacks delivered by the evil one.

The Lord God is our hope and our salvation. Through His Son Jesus, we have life. His mercy never fails.

All glory belongs to our God. Praise Him from the mountains. Praise Him from the hills. Praise Him from the countryside. Praise Him from the ocean. Bless Him and praise Him always. His love endures forever.

God restores our soul.

Do Not Be Anxious

Jesus commanded us not to be anxious about tomorrow, for tomorrow will be anxious for itself. Today's trouble is enough for our mind to resolve, for God will provide us with the strength to overcome whatever ails us. Daily we are to look to God for guidance.

"Do not be anxious, saying, 'What shall we eat?' or 'What shall we drink?' or 'What shall we wear? For the Gentiles seek after all these things, and your heavenly Father knows that you need them all. But seek first the kingdom of God and his righteousness, and all these things will be added to you. Therefore do not be anxious about tomorrow, for tomorrow will be anxious for itself. Sufficient for the day is its own trouble." (Matthew 6:31-34)

We should not worry about the coming days. We should meditate on the present moment as if it were our last. Whatever may be stealing our thoughts is seldom important. Whatever we need is seldom in our thoughts.

If we come to rely on God for all things, He will provide for our needs. We ought not to worry, as worrying brings anxiety. What is anxiety? To fear is to be anxious and not trust God. Trust God and he will relieve the anxiety.

During these troubled days, we have even more reason to give of our hearts to the Lord our God. He promised to look after us and provide for us. There should be no doubt of His awesome and majestic power.

If God could create the universe and everything in it, is our trouble greater that even He could not solve it?

God is beyond the impossible. Do not be anxious.

WEEK 11

Trust in the Lord

Trust in the Lord in all you do, and He will bless you without restraint. His goodness is great, His mercy is sure, and He will give you of His abundance so that you can live according to His will.

> Trust in the Lord with all your heart,
> and do not lean on your own understanding.
> In all your ways acknowledge him,
> and he will make straight your paths.
> Be not wise in your own eyes;
> fear the Lord, and turn away from evil.
> It will be healing to your flesh
> and refreshment to your bones.

(Proverbs 3:5-8)

The Lord is good in all of His ways. He discerns the spirit, gives to the humble and calls the lost into the fold. He gives wisdom to His shepherds and His judgments are righteous. All good things come from the Lord.

Give heed to the Lord's wonderful spirit. Trust in all that He does. He will look after us. He will take care of us. There is no need to worry with the Lord on our side. He will fight our battles and win.

All glory belongs to the Lord our God. His power is from everlasting to everlasting. Let us give of our hearts to Him and He will richly reward us with joy, peace and grace. No one can come between our God and us, therefore trust in the Lord.

Do Good Without Ceasing

Let us be humble in all our dealings, never taking credit for what others have done but giving credit to the one owed. For as long as we do good, our reward in heaven will never fade; whatever we bind here, God will bind in heaven.

> "And let us not grow weary of doing good, for in due season we will reap, if we do not give up. So then, as we have opportunity, let us do good to everyone, and especially to those who are of the household of faith." (Galatians 6:9-10)

Our trust is in the Lord. He knows what is good and beneficial for us as we move toward becoming like Him. When we do good, we are His to do as He pleases. He is the one who will receive the glory and He is the one who will give us the reward.

Let us not grow exhausted of doing good. Our joy comes from doing God's will as Jesus had done when He gave Himself for us. Could we give more than Christ had given? Our will should be God's will, for that is how we grow to become like Him.

Finally, brethren, do not hold back God's spirit from performing a good work with your hands. He will surely bless you for allowing Him to use you in every way He could use you. He is not one to show favoritism to gain advantage. Therefore, do good without ceasing.

WEEK 13

The Lord Will Provide

When all hope is lost is when the Lord will provide the most. He will lift us from calamity. He will lead us away from strife. He will cover us with His power so that we do not need to be anxious in the day of persecution. He will protect us.

> Blessed is the man who trusts in the Lord,
> whose trust is the Lord.
> He is like a tree planted by water,
> that sends out its roots by the stream,
> and does not fear when heat comes,
> for its leaves remain green,
> and is not anxious in the year of drought,
> for it does not cease to bear fruit.

(Jeremiah 17:7-8)

No evil in the world can overcome the Lord. He is good and faithful to His word. He will not let the guilty go unpunished. His judgments are sure, right and just. No one is like the Lord, for His mercies will never fail. His blessings for our lives are provisions for our souls.

Let us not be anxious for all the things that may ail us. We have the Lord's steadfast love to comfort us. We have His faithfulness as an assurance toward the promises to come. No one can come between the Lord our God and us.

In all things, therefore, let us give thanks to the Lord our God; He is good. He will give of what He has and will raise us back to our feet. No matter how painful a trial we face, He will not allow us to stumble.

The Lord will provide.

WEEK 14

Shout for Joy in the Lord

Give praise to God for He is good. He will rescue us from plague. He will deliver us from disease. He will remove us from the presence of illness. Praise the Lord with a joyful shout. Praise His name in all the world.

Shout for joy in the Lord, O you righteous!
Praise befits the upright.
Give thanks to the Lord with the lyre;
make melody to him with the harp of ten strings!
Sing to him a new song;
play skillfully on the strings, with loud shouts.

(Psalms 33:1-3)

Our happiness is in the Lord. He has saved us from the penalty of sin. He has freely given us life through His son Jesus' death on the cross. Our life is His and we are His. All glory belongs to God for His love for us lasts forever.

Let us raise our voices in a joyful shout. Praise God for His protection on our lives. Worship Him from border to border. Give ear to His Word, for it is good and glorifies Him in all things. He gives mercy to the merciful and gives life to the believer.

Lift your hands to the Lord our God, for He is good. He is faithful to His promises and will give peace to us in our time of need. He will always draw near to us. He will never forsake us. His love for us will never fail.

Shout for joy in the Lord.

WEEK 15

Turn to God for Help

Let us pray to the Lord our God for help. He is readily listening for our words. He wants to know us, and He wants us to trust in Him. Through Him, we are safe. Through Him, we will not perish.

> Turn to me and be saved,
> all the ends of the earth!
> For I am God, and there is no other.
> By myself I have sworn;
> from my mouth has gone out in righteousness
> a word that shall not return:
> To me every knee shall bow,
> every tongue shall swear allegiance.

(Isaiah 45:22-23)

From the first breath we took, God was there. He watches over us, making sure we will not stumble and fall. His angels surround us, protecting us in all that we do. We should not fear to have God the Father rescue us. He gave His son Jesus so that we might live.

Let us praise God for He is good. He loves us, guides us and takes care of us in our time of need. Let us praise Him for all His generous gifts. He blesses us with peace, gives us security and leads us through trial, when we need Him the most.

Let us give of our worship to the great and only God. For whatever we are suffering, He will give us rest. His love for us will never grow cold, for His love never fails. He will always look after us, and He will always be there for us.

Turn to God for help.

Do Not Be Afraid

You will hear, "Be afraid, for the end is near. We will suffer and no one will be there to rescue us." Do not believe it, for if there were no God the evil one would destroy the very elect; but we have salvation through Jesus. He is our shield. He is our strength.

> "There is no fear in love, but perfect love casts out fear. For fear has to do with punishment, and whoever fears has not been perfected in love. We love because he first loved us." (1 John 4:18-19)

Illness may threaten us and cast doubt on our lives. Our hope, though, is in Jesus. He will provide us the encouragement to look toward a future filled with joy and happiness. If we believe He is the Son of God, we will live and will not fear of what will happen to us.

All joy is in God the Father and Christ the Son. Floodwaters may surround us, winds may toss us to and fro, but the love of our Lord and Savior will remain firm. He will never surrender us to evil. He will always protect us in the face of adversity.

Disease, be gone, for our Lord is greater. Illness, turn away, for our God is stronger. No power on earth can overcome us. No evil in this world can overtake us. We are Christ's; we are His.

Brothers and sisters, do not be afraid.

I Believe

I believe in one God, the only God, creator of heaven and earth, who made me from the dust of the ground and breathed into me the breath of life. He is the Father.

I believe Jesus is the Son of God, the Christ, the Anointed One, whom the prophets had foretold would die so that I might live; through his sacrifice I no longer have the penalty of sin hanging over my head.

I believe in the resurrection, in that Jesus died on the cross, was buried and after three days and three nights rose from the dead and now sits at the right hand of the Father. I draw my hope from knowing I will one day rise also to stand before God justified.

"By this we know love, that he laid down his life for us, and we ought to lay down our lives for the brothers." (1 John 3:16)

I believe the Holy Spirit is the Comforter God pours into His disciples to bring into remembrance all that Christ had said and done. He lives in me, is a member of the Godhead and is always there giving His church the encouragement to move forward in the face of trials and tribulations. Without Him, I am without purpose or direction.

I believe the church is the instrument into which God calls His elect. Through the church, the world has a vision of what the future will look like once God's government reigns on the earth.

I believe in the elect, whom the prophets had written are those God had purposed from the beginning of the world to reign with God, inheriting all things.

I believe in the Kingdom of God of which the church is now a part, the government of God that will supersede all governments to reign on this earth forever.

I believe the Holy Bible is the infallible Word of God, the book and only book God has inspired, given authority, and is the guide for the church and its calling: to go to all nations, baptizing them in the name of the Father, the Son and the Holy Spirit, teaching them to observe all Jesus had taught.

I believe in miracles.

Rivers of Living Water

Christ Jesus has risen. The Spirit has fallen onto God's people. We are God's people, and we have life through the Spirit. Rivers of living water flow through us as the Holy Spirit lives in us, giving us hope in the resurrection.

> "If anyone thirsts, let him come to me and drink. Whoever believes in me, as the Scripture has said, 'Out of his heart will flow rivers of living water.'" (John 7:37-38)

The good news of the gospel is that we have salvation through Christ's sacrifice. His life made atonement for our sins. We no longer live with a penalty over our heads for the sins we have committed, for God has poured into us His Spirit, and we are now free.

God lives in us through the Holy Spirit, guiding us throughout our walk with Christ. He provides us the courage to give when we do not have, to bless when we are not well, and to show love toward those who hate us. As His Spirit flows through us, we are His.

How wonderful God is to have given His Helper to us the Holy Spirit as a way to change our hearts of stone into hearts of flesh. How great is our God to have sacrificed His life so that we might live. How generous is He to have poured into us rivers of living water.

WEEK 19

I Rest in You, O Lord

There is no darkness in you, O Lord. There is no fear. For you uphold the righteous; you give honor to the humble and you love those who seek your ways. How blessed is the one who looks to you for guidance and strength.

For a day in your courts is better
than a thousand elsewhere.
I would rather be a doorkeeper in the house of
my God
than dwell in the tents of wickedness.
For the Lord God is a sun and shield;
the Lord bestows favor and honor.
No good thing does he withhold
from those who walk uprightly.
O Lord of hosts,
blessed is the one who trusts in you!

(Psalms 84:10-12)

Lord God, you give me rest. Whatever ails me, you comfort me. Whatever threatens me, you protect me. You are my sail. You are my shield. I do not worry when you are by my side. I do not fear. You are a fortress to my life and a bulwark to my heart. There is no one like you, O God.

I rejoice knowing Jesus gave His life for me. He suffered in my stead. He bore my sins and died for me on a cross meant for me. He is my savior, my king and I will always remember what He did for me. I can never forget how He loved me.

You give me peace in a time of turmoil. You provide me strength in a moment of weakness. You are kind, you are gentle and you are loving toward me.

I rest in you, O Lord.

We Have Salvation Through Christ

Living through these difficult days, we have assurance of one thing: we have salvation through Christ. For as disease might threaten us and calamity might surround us, God will hold true to His promise that all those who believe Jesus is the Christ will be saved.

> "God shows his love for us in that while we were still sinners, Christ died for us. Since, therefore, we have now been justified by his blood, much more shall we be saved by him from the wrath of God. For if while we were enemies we were reconciled to God by the death of his Son, much more, now that we are reconciled, shall we be saved by his life." (Romans 5:8-10)

God so loved us while we were yet sinners that He surrendered eternity to live among us and die among us for our stead. Even more so, for as all who are in Adam shall die, so all who are in Christ shall live, since He died on our cross and through no other shall we live.

Knowing Jesus gave Himself for us, we are now to rejoice, to give thanks and to praise God for His gracious gift. For He has blessed us with hope, joy and peace, redeeming us to Him, through Christ, which no one can set aside.

Our hope is in God's grace, and through God's grace, we have salvation through Christ Jesus our Lord and Savior.

The Lord Sustains Us

God will not allow us to perish in vain. His purpose is to sustain us through trial, weariness and disease. He will bless those who look after the poor, take care of the weak and protect the faint of heart. He will restore us from calamity.

> Blessed is the one who considers the poor!
> In the day of trouble the Lord delivers him;
> the Lord protects him and keeps him alive;
> he is called blessed in the land;
> you do not give him up to the will of his enemies.
> The Lord sustains him on his sickbed;
> in his illness you restore him to full health.

(Psalms 41:1-3)

Through the death of His Son, the risen Christ Jesus, God saved us. We no longer are prisoners to sin, but free to live a life filled with joy, brimful and running over. God will deliver us from illness. His promises are sure, firm and right. He will not abandon us.

There will be times we may feel alone, cut off and forgotten. Be not anxious, for our God, our Great God will prevail. When the darkest night sets, that is when the stream of light will appear to provide us with the hope for which we so long.

Give God praise. Bless Him in all things. He will surely deliver us from evil. He will look after us in our time of need. No disease is too great for Him to conquer. Set out to worship Him, for the Lord sustains us.

Take Refuge in the Lord

All glory belongs to God for He is good. No disease shall overcome us; no pestilence shall overtake us, for the Lord is our shield and our strength. He will protect us in all things. Let us take refuge in Him.

> But let all who take refuge in you rejoice;
> let them ever sing for joy,
> and spread your protection over them,
> that those who love your name may exult in you.
>
> (Psalms 5:11)

Let us raise our hands to God and rejoice. He saves us from the perils of this world. He gives us comfort and hope in our hour of need. He pours His love into our hearts and shelters us from harm. His mercy never fails. He guards our way every moment, every day.

Pray and give thanks to the Lord our God, for He provides for our every need. He will not allow us to go hungry. He will restore us in all things. His power is stronger than the most fearsome hurricane. His kindness is as infinite as the deepest ocean. And His love is wider than the great expanse of the universe.

Bless the Lord in our time of trial. Bless His holy name. Give Him praise for all His works. He will not abandon us. He will not forsake us. He will continually strengthen us when we are weak. He will deliver us from evil. Take refuge in the Lord.

God Is Our Healer

There is no illness so powerful that the Lord cannot heal. He commands the heavens, He rules the earth; nothing can surpass God's willingness to bring healing to the one who surrenders the heart to Him.

"In those days Hezekiah became sick and was at the point of death. And Isaiah the prophet the son of Amoz came to him, and said to him, 'Thus says the Lord: Set your house in order, for you shall die, you shall not recover.' Then Hezekiah turned his face to the wall and prayed to the Lord, and said, 'Please, O Lord, remember how I have walked before you in faithfulness and with a whole heart, and have done what is good in your sight.' And Hezekiah wept bitterly. Then the word of the Lord came to Isaiah: 'Go and say to Hezekiah, Thus says the Lord, the God of David your father: I have heard your prayer; I have seen your tears. Behold, I will add fifteen years to your life.'" (Isaiah 38:1-5)

God is faithful in all things. His mercy falls on all who believe. He will not ask us to bear suffering beyond our means. He will not allow misery to fill our hearts. His grace through the shed blood of Christ will save us.

We are His church, and we are those who know joy, for the knowledge of Jesus' sacrifice for our sins fills our hearts with joy. How wonderful God is to have saved us and heal us of our infirmities.

God is our healer.

WEEK 24

God Will Rescue Us

Through our many trials and tribulations, God is there, and He will rescue us. He will not abandon His people. He will cover us with His hand and lead us to safety. His protection will be on those who love Him.

> Because you have made the Lord your dwelling place—
> the Most High, who is my refuge—
> no evil shall be allowed to befall you,
> no plague come near your tent.
> For he will command his angels concerning you
> to guard you in all your ways.

(Psalms 91:9-11)

As these days turn dark and our vision diminishes, let us remember the Lord, for He is good. He will not let us suffer more than we can bear. This life is but a vapor and our true reward is in the salvation the Lord promised through His son Christ Jesus.

Let us be glad and cheerful knowing God has a place prepared for us. Our comfort is in His Word. His Word is a light unto our feet, a provision for our mind and a treasure for our heart. He clothes us in security and provides us with what we need. He will give us the strength to overcome our fears.

We will count on the Lord's wisdom as a standard against plague. His mercy will not fail us. His power will penetrate the very marrow of our being, providing us the encouragement we so truly seek.

In all things, fear not, for God will rescue us.

Our Living Hope

Our hope is a living, breathing hope in Christ Jesus, who died on the cross, on the third day rose from the dead, and now sits at the right hand of the Father. We are free by grace to live a real life, reconciled to God as sons and daughters.

> "Blessed be the God and Father of our Lord Jesus Christ! According to his great mercy, he has caused us to be born again to a living hope through the resurrection of Jesus Christ from the dead, to an inheritance that is imperishable, undefiled, and unfading, kept in heaven for you, who by God's power are being guarded through faith for a salvation ready to be revealed in the last time." (1 Peter 1:3-5)

We should not fear death, for death no longer has dominion over us. God has redeemed us with a price. Our lives are His and the penalty of sin does not bind us, but we live a new life in Jesus.

Blessed be God the Father and His Son Jesus. Blessed be His name. Blessed be His purpose. Blessed be His reign upon the earth as it is in Heaven. Blessed be His church and blessed be the hope we have that one day we will rise to life everlasting.

How great is our God to have given us His life through the Holy Spirit. How wonderful He truly is to have given us our living hope through Christ Jesus.

God's Love Lasts Forever

Though the waves of the ocean beat upon my brow, pressing me to stumble, God's love lasts forever. Though the darkness surrounds me, wanting to swallow me whole, God's love lasts forever. Though my heart plunges in sadness for my loss, God's love lasts forever.

> "We rejoice in our sufferings, knowing that suffering produces endurance, and endurance produces character, and character produces hope, and hope does not put us to shame, because God's love has been poured into our hearts through the Holy Spirit who has been given to us." (Romans 5:3-5)

Though the mountains crumble around me, burying me in its dirt, God's love lasts forever.

Though the winds hurl me about, tossing me to the ground, God's love lasts forever. Though my legs give way to my weakness, I will not surrender, for God's love lasts forever.

God's love is perfect. God's love is kind. It never departs when beaten, never flees when surrounded and never withdraws when sorrow wraps me in its cold grip.

God's love never fails. The mountains will not bury me, the winds will not pitch me, my legs will stand firm, for God's love lasts forever.

PART 2

A Time for Everything

"For everything there is a season, and a time for every matter under heaven."

—Ecclesiastes 3:1

You Are the Great God

God is our Father. He is our king. He created all things, sustains all things and perfects all things through His Son, Jesus. We are His children, loved by Him, protected by Him and nurtured by Him. His heart is in us and we are joyful because of it.

> I will extol you, my God and King,
> and bless your name forever and ever.
> Every day I will bless you
> and praise your name forever and ever.
> Great is the Lord, and greatly to be praised,
> and his greatness is unsearchable.

(Psalms 145:1-3)

God stretched His hand over the waters and gave life to all the earth. The mountains sprung forth, the rivers gave way and the dust surrendered its firstfruits. The stars sang, glorifying His name: Holy, holy, holy is the Lord God Almighty.

Great is our God. Great is His holy name. Great is all that He made. Great is His countenance. Great is His throne. Great is the government He established. Great is our God and king.

How great is the Lord Almighty? Measure the universe from edge to edge and His power is greater. His love overflows, pouring into His creation, giving birth to His children, who will praise Him night and day. Great is our God. Great is His name. Great He reigns forever and ever.

You are the Great God.

God Is Our Loving Father

In all things, God is our loving Father. He begat us, is nurturing us through the Holy Spirit, and is preparing us for our ultimate purpose. We may sin, we may turn away, but God will never forsake us. He will always be there, loving us through everything we do.

> "Beloved, let us love one another, for love is from God, and whoever loves has been born of God and knows God. Anyone who does not love does not know God, because God is love." (1 John 4:7-8)

As we allow God to live through us, love will perpetually flow through us. As God is love, we then will love as He loves. His ways will be our ways and the fruits of His Spirit will be evident in our lives, for our works will manifest His love.

God gave us Christ Jesus as our Savior, our light and our hope. Through Him, we have peace. Through Him, we are whole. Whatever we lack, His spirit lives in us to make us complete.

God is our king, the great Creator, the wonderful Counsellor, perfect in all things, bountiful in all joy and generous in all goodness. His mercy for us will never fail, and His grace will always abound, for God is our loving Father.

God's Gift to Us

Salvation is a free gift that God has given to all who believe Jesus is His Son. No other truth is as powerful, as perfect and as just as that purposed by the Father for our understanding. We cannot earn salvation. God gives it to us freely.

> "For by grace you have been saved through faith. And this is not your own doing; it is the gift of God, not a result of works, so that no one may boast." (Ephesians 2:8-9)

What would we gain if our works were a way to enter into the Kingdom of God? God's mercy would not matter, nor would His forgiveness. Then by what standards would God judge us? If it were so, no one would be worthy of salvation. Thankfully, we have Jesus.

Adam's sin required a blood offering; for through Adam, all have sinned, but through Christ, all shall live. God's mercy is so great that He offered His only Son so that we might live. No longer does sin hold us in bondage, for Christ paid the price for us. We are free.

We do not have to be anxious for the day of salvation. God has given eternal life to us without further qualification. His plan includes us raised from the dead. We are His. He has saved us. How joyful a truth it is to know that salvation is God's gift to us.

Rejoice Always

How wonderful God is to have given us hope through the resurrection. How joyful a truth we have in accepting Jesus as our savior; no greater love had God than for Him to have given His Son as a sacrifice so that we may live.

> "Rejoice always, pray without ceasing, give thanks in all circumstances; for this is the will of God in Christ Jesus for you. Do not quench the Spirit." (1 Thessalonians 5:16-19)

Rejoice always knowing God will one day vindicate us by raising us from the dead. No longer will death have dominion over our souls; we will live forever. His purpose is true, His plan is sure and His justice is swift. There will be no more tears, and we will one day praise Him forever in His presence.

Rejoice always, giving our Lord the praise He so truly deserves. He made all things, blessed us with his presence and gave us His life so that we might draw breath. His light will never go out and His anointing over us, which He has foreknown since the beginning, will be sure, true and just.

Rejoice always with hands raised, for God is performing a marvelous work. He is making a new creation in us. Through His Spirit, our heart of stone has become a heart of flesh, and His joy lives in us always. Great is our God, for there are no other gods before Him.

Rejoice always.

Forgive Always

When God sacrificed His only Son as payment for all our sins, He was showing just how great His love for us truly is. For as in Adam all are dead, we are now alive through Jesus Christ our Lord.

> "If we confess our sins, he is faithful and just to forgive us our sins and to cleanse us from all unrighteousness." (1 John 1:9)

Unless it is a sin against the Holy Spirit, no sin is too great for God to forgive. For God is faithful in His promises, generous in His love, unwavering in His forgiveness, and kind to all. He provides us peace when everything seems to collapse around us, hope when there is no hope, grace when we need it most and joy when sorrow grips our heart.

In the same way, we ought to forgive others as God has forgiven us. Our lives depend on God's mercy, so should we be merciful to others as a way to show them who God is and how His nature lives in us through Christ and by the power of the Holy Spirit.

Of ourselves, we are as specks in the sand. Had God not called us to Himself, we would be nothing. Our repentance through His Son reconciled us to our Father. He has forgiven us and forever we will be part of His eternal family, whose members of His household no one can remove.

Forgive Always.

God Is Almighty in All

When Job questioned God about his suffering, stating how calamity is for the unrighteous, he was really saying that he was righteous and did not deserve what God had allowed upon his life. God had a plan, though. He was there with Job through the trials he endured. For through those trials God was showing his glory.

> Where were you when I laid the foundation of the earth?
> Tell me, if you have understanding.
> Who determined its measurements—surely you know!
> Or who stretched the line upon it?
> On what were its bases sunk,
> or who laid its cornerstone,
> when the morning stars sang together

and all the sons of God shouted for joy?

(Job 38:4-7)

There are moments in our lives when we believe God may have abandoned us. They are only moments; for in everything we suffer, God is showing His glory. Our true test as Christians is our faith we have in the Almighty. Will we abandon God if we did not receive the answer we wanted? The answer is God would never abandon us.

Through His Son, Jesus, we have salvation. God had allowed Jesus to suffer the cross as a way for us to understand God's awesome grace. For through the cross, we also have hope of the resurrection. We will one day live again, and the devil cannot take that hope away from us.

Look to God for salvation and He will give it. Our sufferings are only for a moment, and then God will glorify us just as He did Jesus. For God is almighty in all things.

Our Hope Is in God

Jesus came to save us from our sins. Had Adam not sinned, we would not have need for reconciliation with God. His Son, though, is our salvation, for through Him our sins are no more. God forgave us and we have hope for the coming days.

> "He will wipe away every tear from their eyes, and death shall be no more, neither shall there be mourning, nor crying, nor pain anymore, for the former things have passed away." (Revelation 21:4)

God sees our suffering, He knows what our trials are, and He gives us strength when we feel defeated, power when emptied from our wounds and joy when sadness prevails. He pours more of

His spirit into us so that His eternal joy lives in us. We are invincible with God living in us.

No greater hope do we have than that of knowing God sacrificed His Son as payment for our sins. And if God would do that for us, what lies beyond the grave when He raises us to glory and honor, surpassing even the angels? Indeed, He has blessed us now with utter joy.

Our hope is in the resurrection, from a decaying body to an everlasting one, from a life with an end to living into eternity, and from sadness to utter happiness, brimful and running over. Our hope is in God.

WEEK 34

Gladness in God

Find gladness in God, for in Him is life. He separates the day from the night and there is no sorrow in His presence. His goodness is plentiful for the day and His love for us will never empty.

> For you will not abandon my soul to Hades,
> or let your Holy One see corruption.
> You have made known to me the paths of life;
> you will make me full of gladness with your presence.

(Acts 2:27-28)

We are but a vapor, but in God, there is meaning to all we do. By the salvation we have in Him through Jesus, His son, our sins are no more.

His grace is sufficient to quell our anxious heart. All joy belongs to our Father who is in heaven, and He freely gives it to us.

Look to God for gladness of heart, for He will not hold back His spirit from our bones. He will pour His love into us, so long as we ask with a penitent heart. We will inherit all joy when our deepest longing is to please Him, creator of all things, author and finisher of our faith.

Whatever ails us, let us fear not, for the Lord will prevail. His justice is righteous. Our patience is as a fine fruit He chose for us from the Tree of Life. Our happiness is in our Savior, for He is good, pure and just.

Always seek gladness in God.

WEEK 35

Call to God for Help

Look to God for help. Call to Him, for He is good, righteous and just. He will not allow us to fall. He will lift us from our trials, comfort us with His Word, and deliver us from all adversities. His way leads to life, and He will always keep us safe in the midst of turmoil.

> "Thus says the Lord who made the earth, the Lord who formed it to establish it—the Lord is his name: Call to me and I will answer you, and will tell you great and hidden things that you have not known." (Jeremiah 33:2-3)

Our salvation rests in the Lord. His mercies shall never fail. His kindness toward us is unchanging and everlasting from age to age. He will not forsake us during our tribulation, for no one can separate us from the love of the Lord.

From the beginning, the Lord God of all things foreknew us, instructed, trained and gave us life in Him through Jesus Christ our Lord and Savior. Before His throne, on the golden altar, our prayers burn as incense. Every word we pray is a pleasing aroma to Him.

No one can remove us from the presence of God. He will rescue us from all evil. His hand is against all those who would cause us to stumble. His vengeance is good, righteous and just.

Call to God for help.

The Lord Is Gracious

God gave up His son Jesus so that we might live. His sacrifice opened salvation to all those who call on His name. How merciful He truly is to want to give so much in order to save us from the penalty of sin, which is death. God verily, verily is gracious in all His ways.

> The Lord is merciful and gracious,
> slow to anger and abounding in steadfast love.
> He will not always chide,
> nor will he keep his anger forever.

(Psalms 103:8-9)

God loves us no matter what we have done. There is no sin He could not forgive. He eagerly waits for us to come before him, drop to our knees and confess our wrongdoings. His pardon is from everlasting to everlasting. He remembers not the evil we have committed against Him.

For as often as we come before the Lord and turn away from our transgressions, He will absolve us. Moreover doing so, we become righteous, not because of anything we do, but because God is willing to extend his mercy so that His righteousness makes us perfect.

Oh, how wonderful God is to have given us his grace in such a way that we are no longer dead to sin, but alive with His spirit dwelling in us. All glory belongs to Him, who reigns supreme above all things and blesses us with life.

Truly, the Lord is Gracious.

God's Love Endures Forever

As many stars are in the sky, God's love endures forever. As the ocean is large, God's love endures forever. As many times as we repent, God's love endures forever. For the stars may fail, the oceans may drain, and we may stumble, God's love endures forever.

"For the mountains may depart
and the hills be removed,
but my steadfast love shall not depart from you,
and my covenant of peace shall not be removed,"
says the Lord, who has compassion on you.

(Isaiah 54:10)

As sure as the sun rises and the sun sets, God's love endures forever. The winds in a storm may increase, the earth may shatter beneath our feet, and walls may collapse all around us, but God's love endures forever. We may lose our ability to reason, yet God's love endures forever.

God loves freely, unconditionally and without bounds. His nature affords life to all. Darkness does not exist in Him, for He is light. He bore light at the beginning of the world, and with it, He continues to impart His children with truth. The devil may tempt us, but God's love endures forever.

No trial shall triumph over us, no suffering shall overtake us, and no tribulation shall remove us from our Lord, for God's love endures forever.

His Word is steadfast, immovable and boundless. God's love endures forever.

God Is Our Deliverer

There is only one God and He is the Lord Almighty, creator of all things, without beginning of days, and ceaseless in love. Through His Son Jesus, whom He sacrificed on the cross, we have salvation. All thanks goes to Him, for He is our deliverer.

> I love you, O Lord, my strength.
> The Lord is my rock and my fortress and my deliverer,
> my God, my rock, in whom I take refuge,
> my shield, and the horn of my salvation, my stronghold.

(Psalms 18:1-2)

There are no other gods, for our God is above all. He will deliver us from our enemies, raise us on the last day and we will reign with Him forever. Every knee will bow to Him, and everyone will stand before His throne to give an account to Him (Romans 14:11-12).

No one shall escape God's judgment. His deliverance is at the door. However, let us not judge, for there is only one judge and that is God the Father. He will judge the good and the evil, rewarding the good and casting out the evil into outer darkness.

What are we to do then?

Brothers and sisters, love those who hate us. Bless those who continually curse us. Give to those who take from us, for they do not know they are heaping hot coals on their own heads. Have mercy on them just as God had mercy on us when He forgave us our sins.

For God is our deliverer.

Thanks Be to God

Thanks be to God for His mercy upon our lives, for without it we would not know just how wonderful His love for us truly is.

Thanks be to God, who gives us peace; He has given us the gift of the Holy Spirit, Who guides us in all things pure, good and righteous.

"Thanks be to God, who gives us the victory through our Lord Jesus Christ." (1 Corinthians 15:57)

Thanks be to God, that when evil presents itself, we have a way of escape; His mercy never fails.

Thanks be to God for the joy He shares with His people; storms may gather, enemies may plot, but our delight will always remain in the Lord.

Thanks be to God for He is good; He is gracious and kind toward us, never vengeful or vindictive, always patient and waiting to give us relief.

Thanks be to God, who continually pours His spirit into us, providing strength at our weakest and humility at our strongest.

Thanks be to God, who has chosen us as His elect, showing us His plan of salvation, leading us, through foreknowledge, to what we will become.

Thanks be to God for all the goodness He gives to us daily; there are no other gods beside Him, for He is unequalled, perfect in all things and majestic in His reign.

God Restores Our Soul

God is our shepherd, our bulwark, our awesome strength. In Him, we have everything and lack nothing. He encourages us to rest in pleasant fields where He gives us relief. He takes us by the hand and leads us to calm waters where we find peace.

> He makes me lie down in green pastures.
> He leads me beside still waters.
> He restores my soul.
> He leads me in paths of righteousness
> for his name's sake.

(Psalm 23:2-3)

God shows us the path to walk, which leads to righteousness. All glory belongs to His name. Even in our darkest moment, we will not fear, for He is with us. He is our comfort and our hope. Whatever evil surrounds us will be no more.

God will bless us in the presence of our enemies. The outpouring of His love is generous such that at times we will not know what to do with it all. Our cup will overflow daily with His blessings.

God's mercy for us will never end. His goodness surrounds our lives always. When all else fails, God is there to keep us safe and to lead us to dwell with Him forever.

God restores our soul.

Faith in God

In everything we do, God is there looking after us. Our hope lies in Him, for trials come and go, people can abandon us, places will disappear, but God will always remain the same. His love for us never fades.

"And Jesus answered them, 'Have faith in God'. Truly, I say to you, whoever says to this mountain, 'Be taken up and thrown into the sea,' and does not doubt in his heart, but believes that what he says will come to pass, it will be done for him." (Mark 11:22-23)

Nothing is impossible for God. Through Jesus, we have salvation. Through Him, our destiny is sure. How much more would God do for us if He has already sacrificed His Son in order that we might be saved?

Our trials are only for a moment. We may feel we cannot overcome, but Jesus overcame. We may feel belittled, unwanted and thrown away. Jesus felt belittled, unwanted and thrown away. We may cry out to God, praying that if it were possible that He would remove this cup. Jesus prayed also these things.

Jesus had complete faith in God because He knew God would always rescue Him. Like Jesus, we also have hope that one day all our troubles will be no more. As many times as we fall, God is there to lift us from the ground. He will never abandon us.

Our rescue will not vanish so long as we have faith in God.

WEEK 42

Praise God

God loves us so much. He loves us so much that He gave up His Son Jesus so that we might live. He will always love us more, and He will always give so that we will not be without. His greatest gift to us is the Holy Spirit. For through the Holy Spirit we have found pleasure praising God.

Praise the Lord!
Praise the Lord, O my soul!
I will praise the Lord as long as I live;
I will sing praises to my God while I have my being.

(Psalm 146:1-2)

God has given us so much for which to praise Him. The breath in our lungs, the beat of our heart, the vision in our eyes, the sound in our ears, the taste in our mouth, all come as blessings from Him. He has given us everything, and we did not ask for any of it. He gave it all to us because He loves us.

Give praise to God Almighty, for He is good. He truly is a good, good Father. Wonderful is He. Merciful is He. Love is He. He gives the widow hope, He encourages the orphan, He relieves the sick, and He cures the brokenhearted.

God loves us and will continue to love us until our dying breath. Let us praise Him in all things. Praise Him as we live. Praise Him with outstretched hands. Praise Him in all His Glory. Praise Him, for His love endures forever.

Praise God.

God Is Forgiveness

How can one forgive if love is not in the heart? When a person does us wrong, do we curse them and go on our way? This ought not to be. For as God is love, so is He forgiveness. He forgave us when we repented and gave our hearts to Him. In the same way, we ought to forgive others their transgressions so that we might become as God, filled with love, overlooking another's sin against us.

"And whenever you stand praying, forgive, if you have anything against anyone, so that your Father also who is in heaven may forgive you your trespasses." (Mark 11:25)

When we forgive, we have released ourselves from harboring a grudge. Bitterness is poison to the heart, slowly laying waste our most prized attributes: love, joy, peace, patience, kindness, goodness, faithfulness, gentleness and self-control. Why would we want to hate someone and lose our souls in the process?

God has given us the greatest example of forgiveness when he gave up His Son Jesus so that we might have salvation. No other event is as meaningful as His sacrifice on our behalf. We no longer carry the burden of sin, for Christ alone carried it for us to the cross.

God not only had forgiven us, but He also sent the Comforter, the Holy Spirit, to help us forgive others in the same way. By this, we would become as He is, loving and forgiving, for God is forgiveness.

The Lord Is Our Salvation

King David ran from his enemies yet never failed to honor God. His comfort was in the Lord his salvation. He drew upon God's spirit for strength. He looked to God for hope and rescue. In turn, God the Father, the creator of all things, never abandoned the king. He gave him the power to overcome and lifted David in spirit and stature.

> "He said, 'The Lord is my rock and my fortress and my deliverer, my God, my rock, in whom I take refuge, my shield, and the horn of my salvation, my stronghold and my refuge, my savior; you save me from violence.'" (2 Samuel 22:2-3)

When we believe Jesus is the Son of God, we believe in God's plan of salvation. For Adam fell to sin, and the penalty of sin is death. All have fallen to sin, but God, having given His son as a sacrifice to atone for our sins, rescued us from death. We are free, no longer slaves to sin.

Through grace, God has saved us, not for anything we have done, for there is nothing we can do to earn salvation but by His mercy, He gives it freely. He chooses the weak, the helpless and the maimed and gives us strength, support and healing. And He does it all for His glory.

Our joy is knowing Jesus came down from heaven, sacrificed His life for us so that we can live once again.

How wonderful a gift is it to know the Lord is our salvation.

God's Everlasting Love

God's wonderful nature is unbound. He has set us apart as His sons and daughters to be partakers of His glorious plan of salvation. We no longer bear the penalty of our sins, for Jesus, the Lamb of God, gave His life so that we could live. No other truth is as incredible in depth, as magnificent in width and as breathtaking in height as that of knowing God loves us.

> "Who shall separate us from the love of Christ? Shall tribulation, or distress, or persecution, or famine, or nakedness, or danger, or sword? No, in all these things we are more than conquerors through him who loved us." (Romans 8:35,37)

In every miracle God is there showing His love for those who believe. His powerful presence is in all things He created, for by His spirit He holds all things together for good. Whatever may become of us when we perish will not hold fast. As true as the sun rises, so will we one day rise to stand before the throne of God and marvel at His heavenly countenance.

Had God not loved us, we would not exist. For as we draw breath into our lungs, God is giving us life continually. Our days are as autumn leaves falling to the ground, blown by the wind to disappear in the distance. Yet our hope lies in living once again—this time forever.

Therein is God's everlasting love for us.

WEEK 46

God's Love Is Greater

If we were to take note of all the ways we have loved and of all the times we have loved, our love would be as a drop in the ocean, for God's love is greater. He loved us first, He loves us unconditionally, and there is no bound to His love. God is love.

> "Anyone who does not love does not know God, because God is love. In this the love of God was made manifest among us, that God sent his only Son into the world, so that we might live through him." (1 John 4:8-9)

How powerful a message it is to know that God would give up His divinity so that He could walk among us, experience things like us and die like us. His love for us is so vast that He would choose to die for us in order that we might live.

Every moment we have of breath is a moment closer to being with God. His plan is for us to be like Him: gracious, kind, considerate, gentle, patient, joyful and loving; His spirit in our heart is all it takes for Him to live through us.

If we feel defeated, God's love is greater. If we tell ourselves no one cares, God's love is greater. If our spirit has taken to surrender to forces unknown, God's love is greater. With God's love, we will defeat. With God's love, we will care. With God's love, we will have the spirit to overcome. That is because God's love is greater.

God Is Our Fortress

In our weakest state, in that moment when we are about to do anything to remove a trial from our lives, our only choice is to look to God. He, and He alone, will give us the relief we need to rise from our sufferings and move forward.

> God is our refuge and strength,
> a very present help in trouble.
> Therefore we will not fear though the earth gives way,
> though the mountains be moved into the heart of the sea,
> though its waters roar and foam,
> though the mountains tremble at its swelling.
> Selah

(Psalm 46:1-3)

We have no reason to fear. God is great above all other gods. He is the one and only God. If He can create the simplest of flowers, how difficult is it for Him to rescue us from the sufferings of this present age?

Our hope remains in God the Father, who sacrificed Jesus His Son for the forgiveness of our sins. We should count it all joy to know that our tribulations are for a purpose; and that is to change us to become more like Him every day.

What may seem impossible to us is possible for God. What may seem extraordinary to us is ordinary to God. He takes the weak from the world, imparts His spirit and builds His church. We are of the body of Christ; fashioned of the same countenance; saved by God's grace.

No one other than God is our fortress.

WEEK 48

Blessed Are the Persecuted

Jesus forgave those who persecuted Him. Likewise, we should do the same also; for when we forgive our enemies, God will forgive us. Even more so, He will bless us beyond that which we could have ever imagined possible.

> "Blessed are you when others revile you and persecute you and utter all kinds of evil against you falsely on my account. Rejoice and be glad, for your reward is great in heaven, for so they persecuted the prophets who were before you." (Matthew 5:11-12)

God commands us to rejoice and be glad when we face persecution. Our hardships are as seasons, and as seasons change, so do the circumstances to our hardships. What seems difficult now may one day seem as a distant memory. Our persecution will one day fade.

Every trial we face by the hands of an enemy is one step closer to what God wants us to look like. He is building a new person within us. When we are ready, He will rescue us from the hands of our tormentors. It is a promise our Father will keep. He will not surrender us to anyone.

Outwardly, we may have the countenance of sheep, meek and willing to serve. Inwardly, God has given us the heart of a lion, ready to roar at the face of trial. We may feel weak, but with God's spirit living within us, we are strong. We are of the same unshakable resolve as our Father: to do good to all, even to our enemies.

For then we will have fulfilled our calling, and these words will come to pass: blessed are the persecuted.

A New Beginning with God

As we look to the future, we know two things: first, God will be there for us in this life; second, we will rise again to glory and honor in the next life. Our faith is not in vain, for Jesus promised that in everything we suffer now would not compare to what awaits us in heaven.

> "He will wipe away every tear from their eyes, and death shall be no more, neither shall there be mourning, nor crying, nor pain anymore, for the former things have passed away." (Revelation 21:4)

When we accepted Christ Jesus as our personal savior, we accepted God's promises. Not a one will fail. We believe that. We also believe God's hand will scoop us out of the grave, set us before His throne and comfort us. Our salvation is sure. No one can take that away from us.

We have a new life in Christ. Whatever sin may have ensnared us, God freed us from it by Jesus' death and resurrection. We no longer are prisoners to its penalty. Our hope is in God's grace toward us and His unshakable protection over His people, whom He loves.

In the Father, our new life is complete. His spirit dwells in us, giving us the ability to love our enemies, to feed the poor, to take care of the elderly and to look after the homeless. Whatever the challenge may be, He will never fail us, for we have a new beginning with God.

Joy in the Lord

Take pleasure in the Lord and in all His deeds. He created all things for his glory. Give praise to His name on high, for He is great above all things and wonderfully gracious toward us. His mercy never fails.

> "Shout for joy in the Lord, O you righteous! Praise befits the upright. For our heart is glad in him, because we trust in his holy name." (Psalms 33:1, 21)

God's love for us will endure forever. Through His son Christ Jesus, we have salvation. Through no other name will we rise again. He gives mercy to the merciful and honor to the humble. Our joy comes from loving Him with all our heart.

As many times as we feel alone, God will not leave us. As many times as we feel abandoned, God will not forsake us. His spirit lives in us and He will comfort us. His unceasing love will always warm our heart. Whatever we may be feeling, God is there, helping us along the way.

All glory belongs to God. Every word of worship belongs to Him. May our prayers be as sweet incense and fill the heavens with our heartfelt praise. May we reap joy and gladness with every word that we pray, for God is good and His goodness makes our soul glad.

Let us give thanks and praise, for this is true joy in the Lord.

WEEK 51

You Are My Refuge

L ord God, you are so good to me. Your love for me never departs from my heart. Your joy never leaves me empty. You, Father, satisfy me. My troubles are as ocean waves beating down on me, yet you protect me, looking after me in everything that I do.

> The Lord is my rock and my fortress and my deliverer,
> My God, my rock, in whom I take refuge,
> My shield, and the horn of my salvation, my stronghold.

> (Psalms 18:1-2)

My God, I take comfort knowing you will never abandon me. You will always be there for me.

Your spirit will always lead me to do right. Whatever trials may come my way, you will be my light in the darkness and my compass on the journey. I will not be afraid, for your promises hold true. Not a one has failed.

All glory belongs to you, Father. May the cherubim and seraphim proclaim your mighty name. May all nations bow to your majesty. May nature herald your awesome works. May all peoples give you praise.

Through your grace, my sins are no more. My iniquities are as dust, for you have given your son Jesus as a sacrifice never to blot out my name from the book of life. I will declare your glorious presence in my life. I will give you all the glory, for you are my refuge.

A Time for Everything

King Solomon, the wisest king who had ever lived, once wrote that there is a season for everything: a time to grow, a time to harvest; a time to build, a time to tear down; a time to mourn and a time to dance. With every time that passes, we have a chance to learn more about what God's will is for our lives.

> "For everything there is a season, and a time for every matter under heaven." (Ecclesiastes 3:1)

As we grow as sons and daughters of our Father, we have the opportunity to become more like Him every day. We gain a sense of who God is by doing His will. By listening to His still, small voice, we learn His heart, which then becomes our heart. We will have compassion for those who sin against us, forgiveness for those who wrong us, and mercy for those who hate us.

Our lives will have meaning by the changing of the seasons. For as time moves forward, we will forever learn just how much God loves us by remembering that He gave His only son as a sacrifice so that we might live. Moreover, God's powerful testimony for us is Jesus' willingness to lose His life in order that we might gain ours.

How wonderful God is to look after us in due season. His mercy is awesome and His love for us will never fail. Let us count it all joy to know there is a time for everything.

ABOUT THE AUTHOR

Jack Flacco is an author and the founder of Looking to God Ministries, an organization dedicated to spreading the Word of God through outreach programs, literature and preaching. His message of repentance and forgiveness offers hope for those looking to improve their relationship with others through faith in Christ Jesus.

When he is not writing or ministering, Jack spends his time with his wife and two sons, the youngest of whom aspires to become a missionary. His oldest son, who suffers from autism, is learning about God's ceaseless love for those who follow Jesus. Jack's wife is a Holistic Nutritionist and a graduate of the Canadian School of Natural Nutrition.

Jack and his family live in Ontario, Canada, where they dedicate a large portion of their time participating in activities dedicated to managing Autism Spectrum Disorder.